The Trickster's Handbook

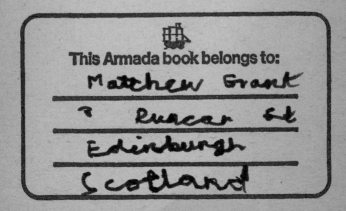

This Armada book belongs to:

Matthew Grant

3 Ruscar st

Edinburgh

Scotland

The Trickster's Handbook

Peter Eldin

with drawings by Roger Smith

AN ORIGINAL ARMADA

The Trickster's Handbook
was first published in Armada in 1976 by
Fontana Paperbacks,
14 St. James's Place, London SW1A 1PS.

This impression 1982.

© Peter Eldin 1976.

Printed in Great Britain by
Love & Malcomson Ltd., Brighton Road,
Redhill, Surrey.

Contents

Pretty Sneaky

1. Inside Out

A book

'I can kiss this book inside and outside without opening it.'

If anyone disbelieves this statement, kiss the book on the cover and then go out of doors and kiss it again. You have now done what you said you would do – kissed it inside and outside without opening it.

2. Keyhole Kate

'I can push myself through a keyhole,' boasted Kate.

Her friends did not believe her so she proved that she could. How? She wrote the word '*myself*' on a piece of paper, folded it, and pushed it through the keyhole.

3. Handy Hint

Can you put your left hand where your right hand can't reach it?

Place it on your right elbow. Your right hand cannot reach it there.

4. Crazy Count

Pencil, paper, rubber

'Nineteen minus one equals twenty,' you announce boldly.

'Nonsense!' cries your arithmetic teacher. 'Nineteen minus one equals eighteen.'

But you can prove that you are correct.

Write down the number nineteen in Roman numerals (XIX). Rub out the I in the centre and you are left with twenty (XX)!

5. Hunt the Thimble

Say to a friend at a party, 'I can put this thimble in a place where everybody but you will be able to see it.'

When he says that he doesn't believe you, put the thimble on top of his head.

6. Sweet Magic

A sweet, a hat.

Place the sweet under the hat and state that you can remove it without touching the hat. Wave your hands in a mystic manner, say a few magic words, and then boldly announce that you have done it.

Someone will disbelieve you sufficiently to pick up the hat and take a look – whereupon you pick up the sweet. You have accomplished exactly what you said for you removed the sweet without touching the hat. You didn't touch the hat – someone else did!

7. Vanishing Sweet

A sweet

This is a neat follow-up to the last trick. State that you will make the sweet disappear 'before your very eyes'.

Then you eat the sweet!

8. Under the Hat

A sweet, a hat

When you have made a sweet disappear you then claim that you will replace the sweet beneath the hat. As you have eaten the sweet, no-one will believe that you can do it.

All you have to do is put the hat on your head and the sweet is then definitely under the hat!

9. Dotty

Pencil, paper

Hand a pencil and paper to someone and ask them to write a small letter I with a dot over it.

Most people will draw this: i. But this is wrong.

A small I with a dot over it should be written like this:

because the lower of the two dots is part of the letter anyhow.

10. Button Up

'I bet that you can't button up your coat in less than a minute,' you say to a friend. He will immediately take you up on this and button his coat as fast as he can go. No matter how fast he moves it is quite likely that he will lose the bet because most people start at the top button and then work their way down. So they have not buttoned *up* the coat, they've buttoned it *down*!

11. Paris in the Spring

Show the triangle on this page to a friend and ask her to read the words on it. Most people will say, 'Paris in the spring'. Is that what *you* thought was written in the triangle? Look again a little more closely . . . It is amazing how many people get it wrong, even on a second or third look.

12. It's Impossible

A book

Show someone a small book and say, 'I can put this book on the floor and you will not be able to jump over it.'

Then place the book in a corner of the room.

13. Foot and Forearm

A ruler, a foot, an arm

'Which is the longest – the length of your foot or the distance from your wrist to your elbow?'

Ask your friends this question and then hand them the ruler so they can measure for themselves. They will be surprised to find that the measurements are exactly the same.

14. Knot Impossible

A piece of string

Challenge a friend to pick up a piece of string, one end in each hand, and then tie a knot in it without letting go of the ends. He will find that it is absolutely impossible.

And then you show how it's done!

Lay the string down on a table in a straight line. Fold your arms and, keeping them folded, pick up one end of the string with one hand and the other end with the other hand. Keeping hold of the string, simply unfold your arms and the knot will tie itself automatically.

15. Keep it Dry

A glass tumbler, a large handkerchief, a bowl of water

Push the hanky into the tumbler and then claim that you can put the glass into a bowl of water and that the hanky will not get wet.

To do this, you first push the hanky well down into the glass and then hold the tumbler upside down. Now force the glass straight down into the water. An air bubble will be trapped at the top of the glass and this will ensure that the handkerchief remains dry.

16. Paragraph Puzzler

Read the following paragraph:

Can you find out what is unusual about this paragraph? It looks so ordinary that you would think that nothing was wrong with it at all. In actual fact nothing is wrong with it. But it is also distinctly odd. If you look at it and think for a bit you may find out what is so unusual about it. Look through this paragraph again, study it thoroughly, and you may find what is missing. Most folk can do it in about half an hour but can you do it in half that? Now can you say what is wrong with this paragraph?

Turn to page 126 and see if you are right!

17. Deep Sea Diver

A glass of water

Boast that you can stay under water for five minutes.

When your friends say that it is impossible simply hold a glass of water over your head for five minutes!

18. The Vanishing Day

There are 365 days in a year. Right? And a year is made up of 52 weeks.

Right? And each week contains 7 days. Agreed?

But $7 \times 52 = 364$. A day must have vanished somewhere!

19. It Doesn't Count

Ask someone the following questions:

'What number comes after ninety nine?'

She will say one hundred.

'What number comes after nine hundred and ninety nine?'

She will say one thousand.

'What comes after nine thousand and ninety nine?'

Most people if asked these questions quickly will now say 'ten thousand'. But they would be wrong. Nine thousand one hundred comes after 9,099.

20. Sticky Book

A book

Hold the book against a wall and say that you are going to make it stay where it is without you holding it. With your free hand you make some mystical passes – but nothing happens.

'Oh, just a minute,' you say, 'I've just remembered something else I need for this trick.' And then you ask someone nearby to hold the book in position for a second or two.

As soon as the other person is holding the book you say: 'There you are! I told you I could get the book to stay on the wall without *me* holding it.'

21. Test Your Reactions

A strip of paper about 10cm long

Hold the paper between the open thumb and forefinger of a friend. Tell him that you're going to drop the paper and challenge him to catch it before it passes through his fingers.

No matter how quick he is he will find that it is not so easy as it sounds.

22. Catch Question

Ask someone: 'Which month has 28 days?'
    If he answers 'February' he is wrong.
    All the months have 28 days.

23. A Year Apart

Here is another tricky question to catch your mates.

'Christmas Day is on 25th December and New Year's Day falls a week later on 1st January, the first day of the following year. If that is normally the case, can you say when Christmas Day and New Year's Day fall in the same year?'

It may puzzle a lot of people because of the crafty way you have posed the question. The answer is, of course, that Christmas Day and New Year's Day are *always* in the same year – New Year's Day at the beginning and Christmas Day towards the end!

24. Breath of Magic

A sheet of paper

Tear the paper into five pieces and place them on your outstretched palm. Now tell your friends that if they choose a number from one to four you will blow the chosen number of pieces off your hand but the others will stay where they are.

When you are given a number you just place the fingers of your other hand on the pieces that you do not wish to move and blow the others off!

25. Upside Down Word

Pencil, paper

Can you think of a word which, when written in block capitals, reads the same upside down as it does the right way up?

One clue – the word has four letters.

Give up?

There is only one four-letter word in the English language that, printed in block capitals, can be read the right way up or upside down. That word is NOON. Turn the book upside down and you'll see.

26. Another Upside Down Word

Pencil, paper

Ask your friends if they can write a word that looks the same upside down as it does the right way up.

When they give up, write the word 'punch', exactly the way it is shown here.

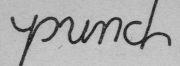

If you turn the page upside down you will see that the word still reads 'punch'. Practise writing the word like this before showing the trick to your friends.

27. Upside Down Word that isn't

Pencil, paper, a mirror

Using block capitals, write the words 'CHOICE QUALITY' on a piece of paper. Turn the paper upside down and look at it in a mirror. The word 'quality' is upside down but 'choice' is still the right way up and perfectly readable!

28. Without moving my lips

A friend in the know

You can gain a reputation for being an expert ventriloquist when you make things talk. And no matter how hard the audience look they will never see your lips move.

In fact, ventriloquism has got nothing to do with it at all, for the voice of the doll or puppet that you use is really that of your friend. You do your amazing act standing near a door and your buddy is on the other side doing the voices!

29. Cutting the String

String, a cup, a pair of scissors

Tie the cup (an old or plastic one!) to a door knob with a long piece of string, as shown.

Now hand your victim a pair of scissors and bet that he cannot cut the string without the cup falling to the floor – and without holding the cup.

When he gives up, cut through one of the loops of the bow and you have done what you said.

30. String 'em along

A long piece of string, two gullible people

Go up to someone in the street and ask if they will help you measure a nearby building. Hand him one end of the string and then walk around the building, unravelling the string as you go.

When you get around to the back of the building find someone else and ask him to help you measure the building. Hand him the other end of the string and then disappear as fast as you can – your victims, after standing holding the string for a while will eventually investigate and they may not think that the joke is as funny as you do!

31. Parallel Puzzler

Paper, pencil

Explain to your friends that parallel lines, because they are the same distance from each other, can never meet and never cross.

Now boast that you can draw parallel lines so that they do meet and they do cross. Challenge someone to try it and when she gives up show her how it can be done – just draw the parallel lines in a double figure of eight, like this:

32. Cork and Coin Conundrum

A bottle with a cork, a small coin

Place the coin inside the bottle and then put the cork in.

Can you now get the coin out of the bottle without smashing the bottle and without pulling the cork out?

Try it before you read any further. Did you manage it? If not, turn to page 126.

Now try it on your mates.

33. Torn Trousers

A coin, a sheet of paper

Place the coin on the ground and hold the sheet of paper behind your back so that it cannot be seen. When someone bends over to pick up the coin, tear the paper – and watch the bender's reaction!

34. Thread Pull, Leg Pull

A reel of cotton, a needle

Place the reel of cotton in an inside coat pocket and then, using the needle, thread the cotton through the coat so that a short length of it lies on your shoulder.

Sooner or later someone will try to remove the piece of thread apparently stuck to your coat. As soon as they pick it up you walk smartly away – leaving your poor victim holding an ever-increasing length of thread.

35. Wet Feet

A plastic bottle with a cap, water, the ability to run away fast

Make several tiny holes in the bottom of the bottle and then fill it up with water. The easiest way to do this is to immerse the whole bottle in a bowl of water. When the bottle is full put the cap on, remove the bottle from the water, and wipe it dry.

Bet a friend that he will not be able to open the bottle without spilling the water. He will lose every time, for as soon as he removes the cap the water will pour from the holes in the bottom.

36. Tipsy Walker

A pair of binoculars, a white line

This is a good one for the playing field or gym or any place where there is a straight line drawn on the ground.

Give someone the binoculars and tell them to look through them at their feet but they must use them the wrong way round. The victim now has to try and walk along the line.

It is not as easy as it sounds. You try it.

37. What is it?

The nerve to do it

Stand in a busy shopping centre staring up at the sky. If you have a friend who is prepared to help you with this joke point up into the air and talk to each other as if something strange was happening up there.

People will soon start to gather around you, all looking to the heavens to see what is happening. When a number of people have congregated you and your friend slip quietly away – leaving the crowd gazing at the sky.

It's an old joke but it's still a good one.

38. The Mysterious Label

A bottle with a label, a pencil, water

People will be intrigued when you show them this bottle for the label is on the inside and not the outside. How could it have got there?

Well, this is how you can get a label inside a bottle. First remove the label from the outside by soaking the bottle in warm water until the label can be peeled off.

Now pour some water into the bottle and lay it on its side. Roll the label into a tube around a long pencil with the printing on the outside. Push the label tube into the bottle and it will open out and float on top of the water.

Next shake the water out of the bottle a little at a time until the label settles against the wall of the bottle. Leave it there until it dries out completely and you have a most curious thing – a bottle with a label on the inside!

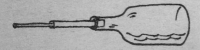

39. Jumping Hat

A hat, an elastic band, two safety pins

Pin the elastic band so that it runs across the inside of the hat as shown in the drawing.

Put the hat on, pull it well down on your head then let go – and it will leap into the air. It looks very funny.

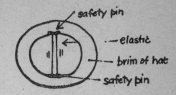

safety pin

elastic

brim of hat

safety pin

JUMPING HAT VIEWED FROM BELOW

40. Jumping Money

A coin, a long length of cotton

Fix the thread to the coin. There are several ways you can do this but a piece of sticky tape will hold the cotton in place quite well.

Place the coin on a path and run the cotton along the ground to a nearby hedge, wall, or doorway where you can hide. When someone stops to pick up the coin, pull the thread and the money will run away from his outstretched fingers. It might be a good idea to make sure that you can run fast too – your friends may not be so amused at your little prank!

41. Nut Case

A nut

Begin by announcing your amazing magical powers, and when you have collected an audience, claim that you will show them something that they have never seen before and that, having seen it, they will never see again.

To prove this remarkable fact you take a nut and, after cracking the shell, remove the kernel which, as it was concealed inside the shell, they have obviously never seen before. Next eat the nut and fulfil the second part of your claim – for, having seen it, they will never see it again.

42. Initiation Ceremony

Two plates, a candle

This is a great joke for a party – provided, of course, that your victim has a sense of humour.

Tell one of the guests that he has been selected to join a new secret society but first he has to go through an initiation ceremony. Light the candle and place it on the table between you. Now hand him one of the plates and you hold the other. He is now to do exactly the same as you.

Gaze at the candle flame; gaze at the plate; rub the *top* of the plate with the fingers of the left hand; rub the fingers of the left hand across your forehead and then down each cheek.

Now ask for the lights to be switched off so that the only light in the room is from the flickering candle.

Continuing the initiation ceremony, with the other person still copying your actions, gaze into the flame of the candle. Gaze at the plate; rub the *bottom* of the plate with the fingers of your left hand; rub the fingers of the left hand across your forehead and then down each cheek.

The lights are now switched on again and everyone in the room, except your victim, will find it difficult to suppress their laughter. Your friend has black streaks across his face! What you forgot to tell him at the start of the ceremony was that before the party started you had blackened the bottom of his plate over the flame of the candle so that when he rubbed his fingers on the bottom of the plate and then on his forehead and cheeks he transferred some of the soot from the plate to his face! He will certainly give you a black look when he finds out.

43. Coin Stuck

A coin, strong glue

Use the glue to stick the coin to the pavement and then stand back and watch the antics of people who try to pick it up.

Of course you will lose a coin every time that you play this trick for you will not be able to pick it up either!

Tests of Strength
and Balance

44. Test of Strength

A telephone directory, pencil, paper

Show your friends a thick telephone directory and boast that you're so strong you can tear it in half.

When you are challenged to prove it, remove a piece of paper from inside the book on which is written the words 'a telephone directory'. Tear the paper in two and you have done what you boasted. You have torn 'a telephone directory' in half.

45. Muscle Power

Hold out your right arm and get a friend to hold your wrist with both hands. Another person can hold your forearm with both of his hands if he wishes. You now say, 'No matter how hard you resist, I bet I can lift my hand and touch my nose.' As you say this begin to lift your right hand and both of your friends will try to stop you. Continue to push against them so that they are now holding on to your right arm as hard as they can.

Then lift the other hand to touch your nose!

46. Escape Impossible

Your friend will not believe you when you say, 'I can clasp your hands together in such a way that you will not be able to leave the room without unclasping them.'

She will believe you when you clasp her hands around the leg of a heavy table or piano. Now she can't get out of the room without unclasping her hands – unless she takes the piano with her!

47. Fingertip Control

Place both of your arms out in front of you, bend your elbows in so that your forearms go across in front of your body, and touch the tips of your forefingers together. Now find the toughest person you know and tell him to grasp your wrists and try to pull your fingers apart. He will not be able to do it. You must be stronger than he is!

48. Impossible Lift

Open the fingers of your right hand as wide as you possibly can and then place your hand on top of your head. Now ask someone to take hold of your forearm near the elbow and challenge him to lift your hand from your head with a straight pull and no sudden movements. No matter how hard he tries he will find that it just cannot be done.

49. Confusing Circle

A piece of chalk, a scarf

Claim that you can draw a circle round someone in such a manner that they will not be able to jump out of it in spite of the fact that they are not tied or held back in any way. One of your friends is bound to respond to the challenge whereupon you bend down as if to draw the circle on the floor. But before the chalk actually touches the floor you suddenly remember the scarf. You use the scarf to blindfold the volunteer and then you start to move him around the room. This, you say, is in order to find the right spot in which the magic spell will work.

Now put your hands around his waist. You tell him that this is necessary to work out how big the circle should be. In actual fact you are really drawing a chalk line around his waist.

Remove the scarf from his eyes, show him the circle you have drawn around his middle, and challenge him to jump out of it!

50. Ball Balance

A rubber ball, candle, needle

You show a lit candle and a rubber ball. Then you blow out the candle and balance the ball on the top of the wick. It looks absolutely impossible – but what the audience do not know is that you have secretly pushed a needle into the top of the candle behind the wick (mind your fingers when you do this). When you appear to be balancing the ball on the wick you are really impaling it on the end of the needle.

51. Blow the Man Down

An empty bottle, a small piece of newspaper

Place the bottle on its side on a table. Roll the paper into a small ball and push it into the neck of the bottle so that it is about two centimetres from the opening.

Now challenge someone to blow the paper ball all the way into the bottle. Much to his surprise he will find that it cannot be done for the harder he blows the quicker the ball shoots out of the neck towards him.

The secret of getting the ball into the bottle is to blow very, very gently.

52. Book Blow

A large book, a paper bag

Stand the book upright on the table and bet your friends that they cannot knock the book over using only their breath. No matter how hard they blow the book remains upright. Eventually they'll say: 'All right, if you're so clever *you* do it.' And this is what you do:

When you originally placed the book on the table you put it on top of the paper bag so all you now have to do is gently lift the neck of the bag and blow into it. As the bag inflates the book will topple over. You have knocked it over using only the power in your lungs!

53. Butterfingers

Two corks

Place the corks side by side on the table and challenge anyone to lift them up together, keeping them side by side, between the first and second fingers of one hand. They will find that it is absolutely impossible because the corks keep rolling over one another.

Although no-one else is likely to succeed, you can pick up the corks quite easily. Bend the first and second fingers before touching the corks and then lift them very gently. Do not press too hard or they will roll. Try this out in private first so that you are certain that you can do it before you show your friends.

54. Straw of Strength

A drinking straw, a small bottle

Can you pick up a bottle with a drinking straw?

You can if you bend the straw about six centimetres from one end and then insert that end into the neck of the bottle. Now pick up the straw and the bottle will come too. A bottle with square 'shoulders' is best for this trick.

55. A Nifty Trick

A playing card, a coin

Balance a playing card on the tip of your forefinger and put the coin on top. With the other hand flick the corner of the card so that it spins away and the coin remains balanced on the fingertip. It may require a bit of practise before you can do it every time.

56. Slide Rule

A long ruler

Balance the ruler with an extended forefinger at either end. Now slide your fingers along beneath the ruler until they meet. When they touched they were both at the exact centre of the ruler, weren't they? It's an amazing thing but it always happens. No matter how hard you try you cannot make your fingers meet at any other point.

57. Elur Edils

A long ruler

Wondering why this stunt has such an unusual name? Well, it's 'slide rule' in reverse.

Place your extended forefingers side by side and balance the centre of the ruler on top of them. Now move your fingers slowly apart. This time you will find that one finger will remain at the middle of the ruler and the other one will move towards the end. Once again, there is nothing you can do about it – it just happens that way!

58. Hands Up

Get a friend to stand in a doorway and to push the backs of his hands against the door frame as hard as he can. Keep him there for at least a minute and make sure that he is pushing hard all the time.

Now tell him to relax the pressure and move away from the door. As he does so both of his hands will rise in the air as if pulled by invisible strings.

59. Test Against Ten

'I am stronger than ten people,' you boast. And you can prove that it is true.

Face a wall and put your hands flat against it. Your arms must be straight.

Now ask ten people to form a line with their arms held straight in front of them and their hands on the shoulders of the person in front. The person at the head of the line puts his hands upon your shoulders.

When you shout 'now', all ten people push as hard as they can in an attempt to pin you to the wall. But, provided that you can hold off the front person in the line you can hold them all because each person is absorbing the effort of the person behind them in the chain.

60. Twice as strong

Two pieces of broom handle, string

This is how you can prove that you are stronger than two of your friends.

Each of them holds a broomstick in both hands. Tie one end of the string to the top of one stick and then around the sticks as shown in the drawing.

Just by pulling the string hard you can now pull the two broom handles together. No matter how hard your friends resist they cannot match your superhuman strength – the sticks come together every time.

61. Flip

A book, some practice

Balance the book on the edge of a table and then strike the underside with the back of the hand. The book does a somersault in the air and then you catch it with the very same hand that knocked it off the table. It takes some practice but eventually you will find that you can even do it with a pack of cards – without dropping them all over the floor.

62. Amazing Balance

A pencil, a penknife

Open the penknife and carefully push the point of the blade into the pencil about two centimetres from the sharpened end.

Now place the point of the pencil on the tip of your forefinger and you will find that it will balance in a most peculiar fashion.

By opening and closing the penknife or by altering the angle between the blade and the pencil you will find that it is possible to balance the pencil in several different positions.

63. Coat Hanger Coin Spin

A coin, a coathanger

Balance the coin on the centre of the bar of the coat-hanger and suspend the coathanger from your forefinger. Now, very carefully, start to swing the coathanger from side to side and you will find that the coin will remain in position. Gradually and smoothly increase the swing and eventually you will find that it is possible to twirl the hanger round and round on your finger and still the coin will remain in position, held there by centrifugal force.

Until you are sure that you can do it every time it is best to practise well away from anything breakable – and other people – just in case you jerk the hanger slightly and the coin flies off.

64. Straw Lift

Five drinking straws

Place four of the straws on the table and give the fifth one to a friend. He is challenged to lift the four straws off the table using only the fifth straw. The straws can be arranged in any way he likes but none of them must be bent or broken.

Unless he knows the secret it will not be too long before your victim admits defeat. You then show him how it's done.

First lay two of the straws parallel to each other and then on top of them place the other two in a diagonal cross. The fifth straw, the one that has to do the lifting, is then placed so that it goes under the first of the parallel straws, over the diagonal straws at the point where they cross, and under the second parallel straw. You should now be in the position shown in the illustration and you will find that when you lift the fifth straw the other four straws will be lifted also.

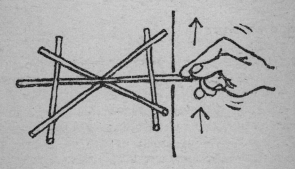

65. You can't do this

Take a sheet of paper and fold it in half ten times.
    Try it – it cannot be done.

66. Balancing Tumbler

A playing card, a beaker

Hold the card upright with your thumb against one edge and your fingers against the other.

Now carefully stand the beaker on the top of the card and at the same time secretly lift your forefinger behind the card to support the beaker at the rear. From the audience's point of view it appears that the beaker is balanced on the card's edge – a fantastic feat of juggling.

67. Card Turnover

A playing card

Place a playing card on the table and challenge anyone to blow at it in such a way that the card turns completely over.

It is in fact absolutely impossible – but you can do it. This is how:

Gently blow the card along to the edge of the table until part of the card sticks out over the edge. Then kneel down and give the card a short, sharp blow from underneath and it will turn over.

68. Coin Balance

A coin, a pound note

Fold the pound note (or a piece of paper if you are not that rich) in half lengthways and then stand it on the table so that it forms a tunnel in the shape of an inverted V. Now challenge anyone to balance the coin on top of it. It is not absolutely impossible but it is extremely difficult to do and most people will soon give up.

There is, however, an easy way to do it – although you will still need a steady hand. Fold the ends of the note inwards so that they form a right angle and balance the coin at the centre of the fold. Now carefully, very carefully, straighten out the note and, with a bit of luck, the coin will remain balanced on the fold.

69. The Spinner

A cigarette paper

Fold the edges of the paper up so that it forms a small box. Place the base of this box against the tip of your left forefinger. As you let go with the right hand move the left hand forward. With a bit of luck the paper box will begin to spin like a propellor.

If you move the left arm in a circle you will be able to keep the propellor going for quite a while.

This will probably take a bit of practice before you will be able to do it, but stick at it because it looks quite spectacular.

70. Ping Pong Pyramid

Three ping pong balls, rubber cement

Your audience will admire your skill as a juggler when you balance three table tennis balls on top of each other. But what they do not know is that before your performance you treated the balls with some rubber cement.

The cement used in cycle repair outfits is what you need. Place a small spot on two of the balls and a spot on either side of the third ball. When the balls are placed together so that the rubber spots touch (the ball with two spots being placed between the other two) the cement will hold them together sufficiently for the amazing balance to be achieved.

71. Cork and Forks

A cork, a match, two forks

Push one end of the match into the bottom of the cork. Now push a fork into each side of the cork and you will find that, by placing the end of the match on your fingertip, you can balance the whole lot quite easily. If you have a steady hand you can even balance the match, cork, and forks on the top of a pencil or even on the end of another match.

72. Flying Newspaper

A newspaper, a ruler

Place the ruler on the table so that five or six centimetres extend over the edge of the table. Cover that part of the ruler on the table with a large sheet of newspaper and challenge your friends to hit the projecting end of the ruler with their fist and send the paper flying through the air.

They will find that it just cannot be done. In fact, if they try too hard, they are more likely to break the ruler than lift the paper into the air!

73. Finger Fun

Tell someone to do this:

'Hold your arms out in front of you with the right palm facing to the right and the left palm facing to the left. Place the right arm over the left arm and then clasp the hands together tightly with the fingers entwined. Next lower your arms, keeping the hands clasped, then bend the elbows outwards and bring your interlinked hands up to your chin.'

When your friend has reached this position point to one of her fingers (be careful that you do not touch it) and ask her to wiggle it. Most people will wiggle the wrong finger.

74. Cutlery Matchic

A match, a table knife, a fork, a tablespoon

Push the knife in between the third and fourth prongs of the fork and then push the spoon into the same gap so that all three are clipped together. Now push one end of the match in between the first and second prongs of the fork. Hold the complete assemblage in your hands and carefully place the head of the match on the edge of the table. The whole lot will balance there. It looks absolutely amazing.

It must be Matchic

Match of the Day →

BRITISH MATCHES

75. Match Piles

A box of matches

Before you read any further go and get a box of matches. Got them? Good. Now follow these instructions:

Empty the matches on to a table. Now think of any number between three and thirteen. Do not tell me what it is. Take that number of matches and place them in a pile in front of you. Now make two more piles each containing the same number of matches as in the first pile.

Have you done that? Right, now you should have three piles of matches in front of you each of which contains the same number of matches. Take three matches from the right hand pile and place them on the middle pile. Now take three matches from the left hand pile and place them on the centre pile. Next count the number of matches in the left hand pile and, whatever that number is, take that number of matches off the centre pile and place them on the right hand pile. Finally take two matches from the centre pile and place them on the left hand pile. Now count how many matches you have left in the centre pile.

Although I have no idea of the number you thought of in the first instance and I have not been watching what you were doing I think that you have seven matches in the centre pile.

How did I know? Because no matter what the number of matches at the start, the answer is always seven if the directions are followed correctly. Now try it on your mates.

76. Star Performer

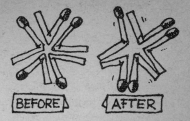

Five matches

Bend the five matches in half, making sure that you do not break them completely in two, and arrange them on a smooth surface in the shape of a ten-pointed star as shown in the illustration. Now challenge your friends to change the match formation into a five pointed star *without touching the matches*.

The answer is really quite simple, when you know how. Just drop a few drips of water into the centre of the star shape and the matches will move of their own accord to form the new arrangement. Isn't that amazing!

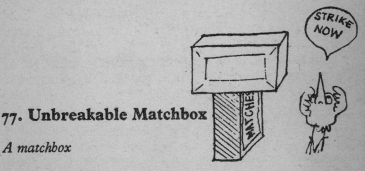

77. Unbreakable Matchbox

A matchbox

Remove the drawer from the matchbox. Stand the cover on the table and then balance the drawer on top as shown in the illustration.

Now challenge someone to break the box by giving it a sharp blow on the top with his closed fist. No matter how hard he tries he will find the feat is impossible because the boxes spring apart as soon as he hits them.

78. Well Matched

Two matches, rubber cement

To balance one match on top of the other is a remarkable stunt which can be accomplished quite easily with the aid of some rubber cement coated over both the match heads.

Move your hand from side to side as if you are attempting a genuine feat of balancing and it will look quite convincing.

79. Straight Drop

A box of matches

Challenge a friend to hold a box of matches about 25 centimetres above a table top and then drop it in such a way that it lands on one end and remains standing. If he does not know the secret he will find that the box simply bounces on its end when it hits the table and then lands on its side.

The way to do it is to first push the drawer open about two centimetres before you drop it. This time, when the box hits the table, the momentum causes the drawer to close up and this ensures that the box remains standing.

First secrete the coin...

80. Match Up

A box of matches, a coin

It is, of course, impossible to know which way up a matchbox will land if you throw it up into the air. But if you secretly place a coin in between the bottom of the drawer and the base of the box it will always land the same way up. This is because the weight of the coin will cause that side of the box to be lower than the other when the box lands.

If you secrete the coin in such a way that the label of the box is always uppermost when it lands you can win a few bets with this one.

81. Animated Matches

Two matches

Place two matches on the table about 14 centimetres apart. When you touch the table in between the two matches they suddenly spring apart as though they are anti-magnetic.

The secret of this trick is very simple but it will fool your friends. When you touch the table top you secretly blow at the table in between the matches and your breath, not anti-magnetism, causes the two matches to move in opposite directions.

82. Which end?

A box of matches

How can you tell at which end of a box of matches the heads will be before you open the box? Impossible? No it isn't – and you don't need psychic powers either. All you have to do is casually balance the centre of the box on your forefinger. Because the end at which the heads are located is slightly heavier that end will dip down and you know instantly where they are.

The more matches there are in the box the easier is this trick.

83. Turn it over

An empty matchbox, plenty of puff

Place the drawer of the matchbox upside down on the table and then stand the cover in an upright position on top of it. Now challenge someone to turn the drawer and cover upside down so that the drawer is balanced on top of the cover – without touching the drawer.

Eventually you will be challenged to do it yourself. Holding the cover in your hand, place your mouth over the cover and suck as hard as you can. This will cause the tray to stick to the cover. Tilt your head back so that the drawer is now balanced on top – and you can now simply put it on the table.

84. Match Stand

A match

When you remove a match from a box of matches and place it on the table so that it stands erect in a vertical position everyone will try to copy your fantastic feat. But they will find that it is not as easy as it looks. Even if they use the very same match as you they will not be able to do it.

The reason why everyone fails is simply due to the fact that you secretly moistened the base of the match before placing it carefully on the table.

85. Multiplying Matches

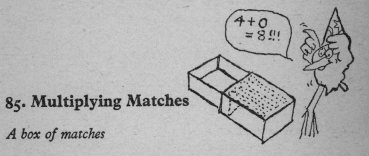

A box of matches

Empty the matches out of the box. Take four of them and put them into the cover of the box. Now replace the drawer a little way until the ends of the four concealed matches are trapped between the drawer and the cover as shown in the illustration. This preparation is made in private before you start the trick.

Show the spectators the box with the drawer sticking out and it will appear to be empty. Place four matches into the drawer and close the box. This will cause the four hidden matches to drop into the drawer so that when the drawer is opened once again there are now eight matches in the box – your magic has apparently caused the number of matches in the box to multiply.

86. Anti-magnetic Matches

Two matches, rubber tubing

Join two matches together by pushing their ends into a small piece of rubber tubing. The sort that you get for bicycle valves is ideal for this trick.

Fold the tubing so that the matches can be placed in a matchbox.

When you want to show this trick, open the box and remove the two matches by holding the rubber. Make sure that the audience cannot see the rubber and make sure that you hold it firmly enough so that the matches do not spring apart.

By relaxing the pressure of your fingers the matches will slowly part as if imbued with a will of their own.

87. Safety Pin Penetration

A safety pin, a match

Cut off the head of the match and then carefully push the safety pin through the centre of the match so that it looks like the illustration on this page.

Hold the pin between the thumb and first finger of the left hand and flick the match with the fingers of the right hand. If the match is hit sharply it appears to go right through the bar of the pin. What actually happens, of course, is that the match hits the pin and then rebounds but the movement occurs so fast that the eye is unable to follow it.

88. An Odd Trick

Three glasses, ten matches

Place the three glasses in a row on the table and put the ten matches on the table in front of them. Now challenge someone to place some of the matches in each glass in such a way that there is an odd number in each glass. All ten matches must be used.

In actual fact it cannot be done.

But you can do it.

How? That's simple – you cheat!

Place five matches in the first glass and five matches in the second glass. Now place the second glass into the third glass so that there is now an odd number of matches in each glass. Ooh, you are crafty!

MATCH WEDGED ACROSS BOX

89. Anti-gravity Matches

A box of matches, a little secret preparation

It looks most uncanny when you open a box of matches and then turn the drawer upside down for none of the matches fall out until you command them to do so.

What the people watching do not know is that a piece of matchstick is wedged across the centre of the drawer. Hold the drawer at the ends between the thumb and forefinger.

To make the matches fall out when you say the magic word all you have to do is squeeze the ends of the drawer. This causes the sides to bow outwards and the wedged match is released, but because it falls with all the other matches no-one will ever know how the trick is done.

90. Rising Match

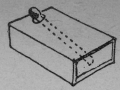

A box of matches

This trick requires some secret preparation. Make a small hole in the top of the matchbox and push a match into it until only the head is showing.

When you need a match for a trick, push open the drawer of the matchbox and the match appears to rise up out of the box.

When doing this tilt the end of the matchbox up slightly so that the audience cannot see exactly where the match is coming from.

91. Matched Bet

A book match, a sweet, a pencil

For this trick you will need a flat cardboard match of the type used for books of matches. Place a sweet on the table and then show the match. On one side of the match draw a cross and on the other side draw a circle.

Now say: 'I am going to throw this match into the air. If it lands with the circle uppermost you win the sweet and if it lands with the cross uppermost you win the sweet.'

Your friend will think you have gone mad for, as far as he can see, there is no way that he can lose.

Throw the match into the air, but just before you do so bend it in half between your fingers as shown in the illustration. Nine times out of ten the match will land on its side and, because neither the cross nor the circle is uppermost, you win the sweet.

92. Match Snap

A match

Can you break a match using only two fingers? It sounds quite easy until you try to do it.

There is an easy way, however. Position the match so that it lies along the inside of your forefinger. Place the thumb of the same hand on the centre of the match. Now simply bend your forefinger keeping the thumb in position and the match will snap.

93. Jack in the Match

An empty book of matches, paper, glue

This is a joke that will make your victims jump. When they open a book of matches out jumps Jack!

You will need a strip of paper about fifteen centimetres long by two centimetres wide and another piece of paper on which to draw Jack's face.

Fold the paper with pleat-like folds about one centimetre apart. Now draw a funny face – or a horrific one – on the second piece of paper, cut it out, and glue it to one end of the pleated strip. Glue the other end of the strip inside the matchbook. Fold up the strip, close the matchbook, and you are ready to spring a surprise on your friends.

As soon as the matchbook is opened your Jack in the Box leaps out.

94. Matches from Nowhere

A box of matches, some secret preparation

The box of matches used for this trick has to be specially made.

Take the drawer of an ordinary matchbox and cut it in two as shown in the illustration. Note that one portion is much larger than the other. Now place the two pieces back into position in the cover like an ordinary matchbox and put some matches into it.

With the larger portion of the drawer uppermost *pull* the drawer out from the top and the matches will stay where they are and the box will appear to be empty. Close the drawer and make some mystic passes over the box. Now open the drawer again but this time *push* it up from the bottom so that both sections of the drawer come up together and the box is now full of matches. It must be magic!

95. Match Balance

A box of matches, a drawing pin

Can you stand a match on a matchbox and keep it balanced there without the match falling over? Well, you may think it's impossible but you can do it this way:

Take a drawing pin and push it through the cover of the box from below so that the point of the pin sticks out from the top of the box.

When you want to impress someone with this fantastic feat of balancing you simply remove a match from the box and, while pretending to get it balanced correctly, stick its 'tail end' on to the pin.

96. The Floater

Matches, a small pin, a glass of water

'Can you make a match float upright in a glass of water?' you ask.

'Of course not!' your friends reply. 'That's impossible.'

You then take a match and drop it into the water and it floats in an upright position!

The secret lies in the fact that the match you use is specially prepared beforehand. A small pin had been inserted into the bottom of the match which will cause the match to float upright. If anyone else wants to have a go make sure that they are given an ordinary match.

97. Match Spread

A saucer of water, matches, soap

Place some matches in a saucer of water in a star-like formation as shown in the drawing.

Now tell your audience that you can make the matches move without touching them and without blowing on them.

All you have to do is touch the water in the centre of the saucer with a piece of soap. Much to everyone's surprise the matches begin to move away from the centre of the saucer.

Just try this – it looks most uncanny.

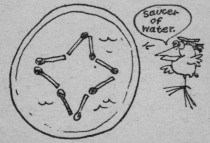

98. Odd or even?

A box of matches, the gift of the gab

Tip the matches on to the table and ask someone to think of a small number and then to pick up that many matches whilst your back is turned.

When she has done this you turn round and pick up a few matches also. It does not matter how many you pick up but it must be an odd number. Now say: 'I can have no idea how many matches you have picked up but if you have an even number of matches and add them to the matches I have in my hand the total will be an odd number. If you have an odd number of matches and you add them to mine the total will be an even number.'

When the spectator's matches and your matches are added together it is found that what you said is correct.

The trick is, in fact, very simple and it works automatically but you must act as though it was a very serious trick to convince the spectator that you are a real magician.

99. Come Together Matches

A saucer of water, matches, blotting paper

This trick is the opposite of No. 97. The matches are placed near the outside edge of the saucer and they are made to come towards the middle.

To do this all you have to do is stick one corner of the blotting paper in the centre of the water and the matches come together.

Another way to do this trick is to pour some sugar into the centre of the saucer.

100. The Rattler

Four matchboxes, some matches, a large elastic band

This trick requires some secret preparation before you show it.

Place the matches in one of the boxes and strap it to your right wrist with the elastic band. (Or a length of string or bandage.) You must also wear a coat or a long-sleeved jumper for this trick so that the secret matchbox cannot be seen. Place the three empty boxes in your pocket and you are ready to baffle your audience.

Take the three boxes from your pocket one at a time and place them in a row on the table. You now explain that one box has some matches in it but that the other two are empty. Pick up the centre box with your right hand and shake it. It will sound as if it has matches in it but it is really the concealed box on your wrist that is making the noise. Now mix the three boxes together and ask someone to pick out the full box.

Whichever one he picks he will be wrong for you can make any of the three appear to contain matches by picking it up with the right hand. If you want a box to be empty you pick it up with the left hand.

101. Indestructible Match

Two matches, a handkerchief

Before showing this trick to anyone, secretly push one of the matches inside the hem of the handkerchief. Place the hanky in your pocket along with the second match and you are ready to perform.

When someone asks to see a trick take the match from your pocket and allow the spectators to examine it. When the match has been returned to you cover it with the hanky. Now say that you are going to break the match through the material but you really break the one concealed in the hem. The spectators will hear the snap and assume that you have broken the match they examined.

Now say some magic words and show the match to be completely unharmed as you casually replace the handkerchief in your pocket.

Fantastic Feats
with Food and Drink

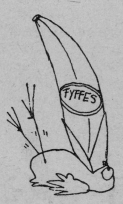

102. Egg Stand—1

An egg

Challenge your friends to stand an egg on one end. They will not be able to do it (unless, of course, they have a copy of this book!) You then show them how.

Shake the egg vigorously for a minute – wait a second or two – and then place it carefully on its broadest end on a table that has a cloth on it. The egg will stand there . . . Amazing!

103. Egg Stand—2

An egg, some salt

Here is another way to stand an egg on end. This time you do not have to shake it.

In your left hand you have a small supply of salt. The egg is on your right hand.

Pretend to cough and bring your right hand up to cover your mouth. As you do this, secretly stick out your tongue slightly and wet the end of the egg.

Now place the egg into your cupped left hand for a second or two so that some of the salt sticks to the dampened end. Next place the egg on to the tablecloth. As you do this just twist the egg once or twice. This twisting action is very important because it makes the salt form into a nest that supports the egg. Leave go very carefully and the egg should stand upright.

Now pick up the egg and hand it to someone else to have a go. But as you hand the egg over you sneakily remove the salt so that the egg will not stand for anyone else.

Practise this trick a few times before showing it to anyone.

104. Glow Worm

Two sugar lumps

This is a clever way to make a glow in the dark. All you need is two lumps of sugar which you rub together slowly and hard and they produce the glow. It looks quite eerie.

105. Fruity Fangs

A piece of orange peel

Frighten your family with a set of fangs that any monster would be proud of. All you need is a piece of oval-shaped orange peel large enough to fit over your teeth.

Cut out some super fangs and pop the peel into the front of your mouth between your lips and your teeth. Now take a look in the mirror and give yourself a scare.

Happy hauntings!

106. Eggstraordinary!

A hard-boiled egg, a pin, a candle, a glass of water

You show your friends a silvery-coloured egg which is in a glass of water. 'I will now make the egg change colour,' you boast and you remove the egg from the water. When you show it to your audience they are surprised to see that it is now black – but as soon as you drop it into the water once again it changes back to silver.

This is how you do it. Get a hard-boiled egg and stick a pin into it. Using the pin as a handle hold the egg over the flame of a candle until the shell is completely blackened. When this blackened egg is placed in water it will appear to be silver but when out of the water it becomes black. Isn't that amazing?

107. Iceberg Elevation

An ice-cube, a glass of water, a piece of string, salt

Place the ice cube in the glass of water and challenge someone to lift it out with the string. And to make it even more difficult tell them that they must not touch the glass, the ice, or the water with their fingers.

When everyone has given up, you rest the centre portion of the string upon the ice. Then you sprinkle some salt over the string and the ice cube. Wait for a few seconds and then lift both ends of the string. Lo and behold the string is now stuck to the ice and the cube is easily lifted from the water and out of the glass!

108. Salt Cellar Suspension

A salt cellar, a match

Conceal a match, or a toothpick, in one hand and show a salt cellar with the other. Place the tip of the forefinger, with the match hidden behind the finger, on top of the salt cellar and secretly push the stick into the hole at the top of the cellar.

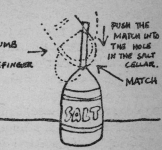

From the front it looks as if the salt cellar is suspended from your finger tip.

109. Egg Spinner

A bowl of eggs, a hard-boiled egg, a dinner plate

You take an egg out of the bowl and spin it like a top on the dinner plate. To do this, hold it between the palms of each hand and then move one hand quickly forward and the other one backwards, leaving go of the egg at that point to make it spin. If you are really clever you may be able to spin the egg using only one hand by flicking your fingers.

Now each of your friends take an egg but they cannot make them spin. Do not, of course, tell them that yours was the hard-boiled egg (put a secret mark on it so that you pick the right one). A raw egg will not spin.

110. Thanks for the drink

Two glass tumblers, water, a chin

Fill one of the tumblers with water and then place the empty glass on top of it. Now challenge anyone to drink the water from the bottom glass without touching either glass with his hands.

You can, of course, do it, and this is how:

First pick up the uppermost tumbler by gripping it between your chin and your chest. Then pick up the lower glass in your teeth and tilt your head back so that you can drink the water.

It is a trick that will require a bit of practice before you show it to anyone but it is well worth the effort involved.

111. Fortune-telling Banana

A banana

Ask the banana a question.

Now cut off the end furthest from the stalk and look at the centre of the pulp. If it looks like a Y the answer to the question is 'yes'. If it looks like a dot then the answer is 'no'.

If the central, dark portion of the banana is any other shape then the answer to your question is 'maybe'.

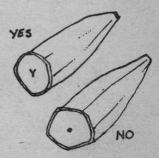

FORTUNE TELLING BANANA

YES

NO

112. Floating Sausage

Two fingers

Have you ever seen a sausage floating in the air? What, never? Well, do this and you will.

Hold the tips of your forefingers together in front of your eyes. Now look beyond your fingers at something in front of you. As you do this you will see a sausage appear between the fingertips. Do not focus your eyes on the fingers or the sausage will disappear. Move your fingers apart and the sausage will appear to be floating in mid-air.

Next time someone asks, 'Have you ever seen a floating sausage?' you'll be able to reply, 'Yes, I have!'

113. Floating Egg

Two glasses of water, an egg, some salt

Hand someone one glass of water while you hold the other. Show the egg and ask the spectator to put it into his glass of water so that it floats. As you say this you demonstrate what has to be done by putting the egg into your glass, where it floats.

Hand the egg to the other person, but when he puts it in his glass the egg sinks to the bottom. The egg will float in your glass but not in his.

The secret of this trick is that the glass of water you hold is not so innocent as it appears. It has a large quantity of salt dissolved in it, which will support the egg, but the spectator's glass contains ordinary water.

114. Bottling an Egg

An egg, a milk bottle, string, matches

Johnny Joker was the envy of his classmates for on his desk he had a milk bottle with a hard-boiled egg inside it. And yet the egg was larger than the neck of the bottle. It puzzled everyone who saw it for no-one could work out how he'd managed to get the egg into the bottle.

Here is Johnny's secret.

First he dropped a piece of burning string into the bottle. Then he placed a hard-boiled egg on the top of the bottle. As the flame burned all the oxygen in the bottle it caused a vacuum and this sucked the egg inside. As the egg began to move magically into the bottle he turned the bottle on to its side so that the egg would not drop to the bottom and crack. Then he carefully rinsed out the bottle so that there was no trace of the burnt string and no clue as to how he had done this amazing thing.

115. Another Egg in another Bottle

One egg, vinegar, a milk bottle

This is an easier way to get an egg into a milk bottle but it requires a bit of patience. All you have to do is soak the egg in vinegar until the shell becomes so soft that you can simply push the egg into the bottle. Rinsing the bottle out with cold water will remove the smell of vinegar and make the shell hard again.

116. Bottled Fruit

A milk bottle, string, an apple tree, lots of patience

Freda Fishface goes to the same school as Johnny Joker and she spent several days trying to work out how he got that egg into the bottle. She never did solve the problem but she was determined to go one better. Later in the term she pranced into the classroom with a large smile on her face. In her hand she held a milk bottle inside which there was a juicy-looking apple. The apple was so big it was squashed up against the sides of the bottle!

Freda's secret of how she got the apple into the bottle was rather clever.

When the apples on the apple tree in her garden were still quite small, Freda selected one that was near the end of a branch and pushed it, complete with the branch, into the bottle. Then she used some string to tie the bottle securely to the branch and she left it there until the apple was fully grown.

When the apple was ripe, Freda got her father to cut off the twig holding the apple inside the bottle, as close to the apple as he could.

Hey presto – a bottled apple!

117. Apple Catch

An apple, a nut, a paper tube

From a sheet of paper or thin card make a tube that is just large enough to cover your apple. Take the apple and scoop from its base a hole large enough to accommodate the nut. Put the nut in the hole and you are ready to catch someone.

Show a friend the apple (keeping the nut in place and hidden from view) and state that you are going to test the speed of his reactions. Put the apple on the table and cover it with the tube. Say: 'When I say "go", I will lift this tube and then put it down again. I bet you can't scoop the apple off the table before I put the tube back over it.' As you are saying this you lift the tube a couple of times to explain what you mean.

As soon as your friend accepts the challenge, cover the apple again and tell him to get ready. Call out, 'One, two, three – go' – and lift up the tube but hold the apple through it so that the apple is lifted also and the nut is left on the table. Your friend will go to scoop the apple away but he will have quite a shock when he sees that it has changed to a nut!

118. Personal Fruit

An apple on the tree, sellotape, patience

Freda's not the only one who takes apples to school.

Anne often does – and she always knows which is hers because it has her name emblazoned on its skin. Everyone is puzzled as to how she gets her name on the apple but if they looked in her garden they might find the answer.

Whilst the apple is still growing she cuts out pieces of sticky tape and puts them on the apple to form her name. When the apple is ripe she picks it and then removes the tape and the area underneath the tape is bleached with her name.

If you have an apple tree, you can grow named apples for each member of the family.

119. How to Eat a Candle

A banana, an almond

To the audience watching this trick it appears that you are eating a candle but if you look at the things you need for the trick you will see that in fact a candle is not one of them. The object that looks like a candle is simply a piece of banana with a small piece of almond for a wick.

To make the effect more realistic you will find that it is possible to light the almond nut wick and it will burn just like a real candle. Blow out the flame and eat it as though eating a candle was the most natural thing in the world.

120. Fantastic Fruit

An apple, an orange, a sharp knife, a spoon, a handkerchief

Here's a fruity trick with which you can baffle your friends.

Very carefully, cut the peel of an orange as shown in the drawing. Now, using the spoon, scoop out the fruit and then leave the skin until it is dry inside.

Place an apple inside the orange peel.

Hold the orange peel closed so that it looks like an ordinary orange and show it to your friends. Say, 'I don't like oranges,' and cover it with your handkerchief. Wave your hand over the hanky as you recite the magic words: 'Abracadabra. In magic I'll dabble, to change this orange into an apple.' As you say the word 'apple', whisk the handkerchief away with the orange peel concealed inside it.

Casually put the handkerchief (and the peel – but no-one sees this) into your pocket and take a bite of the apple.

121. Banana Split

A banana, a needle, thread

When you tell people that you can slice a banana by magic they may not believe you. But when you peel it they will have to believe you for the fruit is already sliced, just as you said.

This trick requires some secret work beforehand and this is what you have to do. Thread a needle with some cotton and then push the needle into the skin of the banana and out again a short distance away. Now push the needle back into the same hole and out somewhere else. Keep doing this all the way round the banana until you come back to the first hole. Pull both ends of the thread away from the banana and you will have sliced the fruit without removing the skin. Repeat this action at several places along the banana so that when it is eventually peeled the slices will fall on to the table.

122. Sliced Apple

An apple, needle, thread

With a bit of patience it is possible to prepare an apple in exactly the same way as the banana in 'banana split'. An apple prepared in this way provides a convincing demonstration of your strength, for when you hit it with your hand it splits into two. Some kung fu experts chop wood with their hands – you chop apples!

FIG. 1

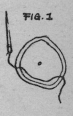

FIG. 2.

FIG. 3.

123. The Ghost is Thirsty

A glass of water, sellotape, a straw

Put some water in the glass and then stick several strips of the tape across the top of the glass so that it is absolutely impossible for anyone to drink the water.

State that you are going to call upon the family ghost but first the lights must be switched off. After a few seconds you call for the lights to be switched on again. The ghost has certainly made a visit for the glass is now empty – but the tapes are still in place.

As you may have guessed, it is not a ghost but you who drinks the water. When you tape up the glass you make sure that there are some small gaps left open. As soon as the lights are out you remove a drinking straw from your pocket, push it into one of the gaps in the sticky tape, and suck up the water.

Hide the straw in your pocket again and have the lights switched on to prove that the family ghost really has paid a visit.

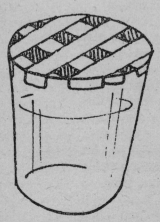

how exstrawdinary

124. Drink it up

Two glasses, a soup plate, some water, a drinking straw

First you must have two glasses full of water, one of which is inverted and placed on top of the other. The easiest way to do this is to fill a large bowl with water and position the tumblers under the water before bringing them out and placing them on the soup plate.

Now challenge anyone to drink the water from the inverted glass tumbler without touching either of the glasses.

If you have read the list of requirements at the beginning of this trick you may have already guessed the answer. You need a drinking straw. Put the straw in your mouth and place the other end at the point where the two glasses touch. Suck through the straw and the water will be sucked out from the uppermost glass. It is possible that some of the water may spill out – so don't do this trick without the soup plate!

125. Coffee Break

A glass tumbler, black coffee, water, a piece of cardboard, a straw

You show your audience a jug of coffee and a jug of water. Then you say: 'Can you pour the coffee into this glass, then pour the water in, and then remove only the coffee?'

Like most of the tricks in this book it sounds absolutely impossible but it is really quite easy when you know how.

First pour the coffee into the glass. (If the coffee is hot put a spoon in the glass to absorb the heat or the glass may break.) Now take a disc of cardboard which you float on top of the coffee. You didn't tell anyone about the disc of cardboard, did you? – you crafty thing. The diameter of the disc should be slightly less than the diameter of the inside of the glass.

Now pour the water slowly, and very carefully on top of the cardboard disc and it will seap over the card and on to the coffee but the two liquids will not mix. You can now remove the cardboard.

Now take the straw from your pocket (something else that you did not tell your audience about) and place it into the bottom of the glass. Now suck the coffee out until only the water remains and you have separated the two liquids.

you never told anyone about the disc of cardboard, – did you ?

cheat

Miracles of Mindreading

126. Sleight of Foot

Pencil, paper

State that you can read people's minds, then ask someone to write something on a sheet of paper, put it on the floor and stand on it.

'I will now tell you what is on the paper. Just let me concentrate for a second. Ah, yes, I can see it now. It's your foot!'

127. No!

Paper, pencil

Say that you will transmit your thoughts to someone.

Write on the paper the word 'No', but do not let anyone see what you have written.

Ask someone if he knows what is written on the paper. When he says 'No', you shout, 'That's absolutely correct!' and turn the paper round to show what you wrote.

128. The Very Same Word

Paper, pencil

A spectacular feat of mindreading! Get a friend to write down any word on a piece of paper. You state that you will write the very same word on another piece of paper even though you could not possibly have seen what the person wrote.

The spectator calls out the word of which he is thinking. You then hand him your piece of paper saying: 'Will you please confirm that even though I did not see what you had written I have written the very same word.' The spectator reads what is on the paper and agrees that your statement is correct.

What did you write on the paper? That's simple! You wrote: '*The very same word.*'

129. Muscle Reading

A friend who knows how the trick is done

While you are out of the room the audience decides upon any three-figure number. You come back into the room, place your fingers upon your friend's temples (to pick up his brain waves), and reveal the number that everyone is thinking of, even though not a word has been spoken.

This is how you do it. When you place your fingers on your friends' temples he tightens his jaw for the appropriate number of times, allowing a pause between each of the three numbers. This tightening of the jaw can be felt at the temples – try it and see how easy it is. Thus, if the audience decides upon the number 342 your friend clenches his jaw three times, pauses, then four times, pauses again, and then clenches his jaw twice. You now know that the selected number is 342.

130. That's It!

A friend who knows how the trick is done

This is a good trick for a party.

While you are out of the room the others choose an object in the room. When they have decided they call you back.

Your friend starts to point to things around the room. As soon as he points to the chosen object you say, 'That's it!'

How did you know which was the chosen object? Before the party you and your friend agree that just before he points to the chosen object he will point to something beginning with the letter C. The next thing he points to will be the thing chosen by the spectators.

As there are usually several things in a room that begin with C, you can do this trick several times without anyone discovering the secret.

131. That's It Again

A friend who knows how the trick is done

This trick is rather like the last one but this time anyone can do the pointing.

Before the party you and your friend agree that when the chosen object is pointed to he will give you a secret signal.

This signal must not, of course, be too obvious or everyone will know how the trick is done. A simple signal would be for him to have his hand in his pocket. When the chosen object is pointed to he takes his hand out of his pocket and you will know what was chosen.

Try not to make it too obvious that you are watching your friend or you will give the game away.

132. Heads or Tails?

A coin, a friend who is in on the trick

Several people gathered around a table spin a coin on its top. Even though the magician, that's you, is seated on the floor under the table he can always tell which side of the coin, heads or tails, is uppermost when it has finished spinning.

The magician knows which way up the coin is because one of the people at the table is his accomplice. When the coin falls with the head uppermost the magician's partner raises his right foot slightly. If the coin shows tails he raises his left foot. When doing this your partner must make sure that only the front of his foot is raised and that his heel remains on the ground so that the others at the table will not see his legs move.

last gasp

The Queen of Spades

(died from shock)

133. Your Card

A pack of cards

You shuffle the pack and invite someone to take a card, any card, look at it and remember it, and then replace it on the top of the pack. The cards are then cut several times so that the chosen card is well and truly lost in the pack. You now look through the pack and name one card – it is the very card that the person selected.

You find out the name of the selected card very easily. When you have finished shuffling the cards at the beginning of the trick you secretly look at the bottom card of the pack. A card is then selected and returned to the top of the pack and the cards are cut several times. The first cut brings the chosen card next to the one that you saw at the bottom of the pack. No matter how many times the pack is cut (do not shuffle them) the two cards will stay together. All you now have to do is look through the cards looking for the one you saw earlier and the card below it will be the spectator's card.

134. Psychic Vision

A special blindfold

'My friend,' you tell your audience, 'possesses strange and remarkable powers. He can read a person's thoughts.'

To prove this amazing claim you blindfold your friend and then ask for objects from the audience.

'What's this?' you ask as you hold up a playing card. 'It's a playing card,' says your friend. 'And I think it is the five of clubs.' It is the five of clubs! Then you borrow a pencil and hold it up. 'What's this?' 'It's a pencil . . . a red one.'

And so the act continues and the audience will be completely baffled – until your friend turns his head too much to one side and the bafflement turns to amusement when they realise that the blindfold has a hole in it so that your friend can see everything that you do!

PROFILE

FRONT VIEW

135. Extra Sensory Perception

A pack of cards, a large box, a paper clip

Shuffle the pack of cards and then ask four or five people to each select a card. While they are looking at their cards put the rest of the pack on the table and secretly pick up the paper clip. Collect the cards face down (so that you cannot see what they are) from the audience and hold them together in one hand. In actual fact you have really put them all into the paper clip. Pick up the pack and shuffle the selected cards into it but unbeknownst to the audience the paper clip is keeping all the chosen cards together.

Drop the pack into the box and shake the box to mix the cards even more. Put your hand into the box, find the clipped cards, and then ask the first person for the name of the card that he chose. As soon as he tells you, pull the first card from the clip and show it to be his card. Repeat this with the other spectators and then remove the pack from the box at the same time secretly removing the paper clip so that there is no clue as to how you accomplished this fantastic feat.

83

136. Magic Addition

Pencil, paper

Ask someone to write down any three-digit number in which the first and last digits differ by at least two. Reverse the number and subtract the smaller one from the larger. Now reverse the digits of the answer and add them to the answer. When he has done this he calls out the total '1089'. You then pick up a piece of paper that has been on the table all the time, turn it over, and show a message that you wrote earlier. '*The number you arrive at will be 1089.*'

How did you know? That's easy – the answer is always 1089! Here is an example to show you how it works:

Take any three digit number with the first and last digits differing by at least two:	481
Reverse the digits:	184
Subtract the smaller from the larger:	297
Reverse the digits of the answer:	792
Add the two together:	1089

It works every time.

137. Cups of Mystery

Three bottle tops, a coin, a hair, sellotape

Using the sellotape, stick the hair to the coin as shown in the illustration. This must be done before you show the trick for the audience must not be aware that there is anything unusual about the coin you use.

When the time comes for your performance, place the coin on the table with the sticky tape underneath so that the audience do not see it. Now turn your back and ask someone to pick up one of the bottle tops, place it over the coin, and then mix the bottle tops around until no-one knows which one hides the coin.

When you turn round you simply look for the hair sticking out from beneath one of the bottle tops which tells you where the coin is hidden. The audience, not knowing about the hair, will have no clue as to how you were able to find the hidden coin.

HAIR REVEALS LOCATION OF HIDDEN COIN.

138. Magic Breath

Washing-up liquid, a window pane

This is a good way of revealing the answer to a problem when you know what the answer is going to be before you start. It would, for example, make a good finish to *Magic Addition*. In this case you know that the answer is going to be 1089 so this is what you do:

Get some washing-up liquid on the tip of your finger and use it to write the numbers on the window. After a short while it will be more or less invisible.

When the time comes to do the trick you simply breathe on the glass and the numbers will appear by magic.

139. It Must Be Mindreading

With this trick you can tell someone how old he is and how much money he has in his pocket. You have to be good at mental arithmetic though, for this is how it works:

Ask someone to think of their age, double it, add five, and then multiply the answer by fifty. To his total he adds the number of pence he has in his pocket (this figure must be less than 100 to make the trick work). He now tells you the answer and you can say how old he is and how much change he has in his pocket.

To do this you simply take 250 from the answer he gives you and the first two figures of your answer is his age and the second two numbers indicate the amount of money in his pocket.

Here is an example to show how it works:

Your friend thinks of his age	13
He doubles it	×2
	26
Then he adds five	5
	31
Then he multiplies the answer by 50	×50
	1550
He adds the amount of pence in his pocket	47
And he tells you the answer	1597
You take his answer	1597
And, in your head, take away 250	−250
	1347

The first two numbers tell you that he is thirteen and the second two tell you that he has forty-seven pence in his pocket.

140. Think of a number

Think of a number – any number you like but you will have to do some arithmetic in a minute so you may find it easier if you choose a number less than ten.

Have you thought of a number? Good. Now double it. Next add twelve. Now divide your total by two and when you have done that take away the number you first thought of.

Have you done that?

Now concentrate on the answer and, although I can have no idea of the number you thought of I believe that you are now thinking of the number six. Am I correct? Yes, I thought I would be because if the above steps are followed correctly the answer is always six!

If the above steps are taken correctly . . .
the answer is always 6

mental exhaustion

141. The Mystic Nine

A pack of playing cards, pencil, paper

With this trick you can apparently predict what someone will do before he does it. First you write something on a piece of paper which you fold and place on the table in full view. Then you put three piles of cards face down on the table and ask someone to pick any one of the three piles. When he has made his selection he opens the paper and it proves that you knew in advance which of the three piles he was going to pick.

This is how you do it: Write on the piece of paper, '*You will choose the nine pile*'. Now lay out the three piles of cards. The first pile has four cards – the four nines; the second pile consists of three cards – a five, a three, and an ace; and the third pile contains nine cards. So whichever pile the spectator picks your prediction appears correct – for pile one has four nines, the cards of pile two add up to nine $(5+3+1)$, and the last pile has nine cards in it.

It is very simple – but very baffling to your audience.

142. Booked Thoughts

Two books, both the same

You hand someone a book and then leave the room. From the other side of the door you instruct the person to open the book at any page and read, to himself, the top line on that page.

'What page did you choose?' you ask.

As soon as he tells you the page number you tell him what the top line is on that page.

This is a most baffling trick but the secret is very simple. You have another copy of the book in your pocket. As soon as the spectator tells you his page number you quickly turn to that page and read out the top line.

Do not forget to put the book back in your pocket before you return to the room!

I'M BAFFLED

143. The Three of Diamonds

A pack of cards, an envelope, paper, pencil

Before your performance, write on the paper, '*You will choose the three of diamonds*' and then seal it in the envelope. Put the three of diamonds in the ninth position from the top of the pack and you are ready to start.

Hand the envelope to someone, saying that it contains your prediction of something that is about to happen. Now show the pack of cards and ask for any number between ten and twenty.

Count the chosen number of cards face down on to the table. Put down the rest of the pack and pick up the small pile of cards. Now say: 'We will add the digits of your chosen number and deal that number of cards from the pack.' Thus, if the chosen number was 13 you deal four cards (1+3) from the top of the pack, if it was 17, 8 cards, if 15, 6 cards, and so on. The next card on the top of the packet will be the chosen card. When it is turned over it is seen to be the three of diamonds and when the envelope is opened you are seen to be correct.

You do not, of course, need to use the three of diamonds every time as long as the card you decide upon is placed ninth from the top of the pack before you start.

144. Psychological Number—1

Paper, pencil

Write the numbers 1, 2, 3, 4 in a column on one side of the paper. Show the back of the paper to the audience and say that there are some numbers on the other side. Say: 'In a second I will show you the numbers for a moment or two and I want you, as quickly as you can, to think of one of the numbers.' Show the numbers for a short while and then place the paper down on the table.

You now say, 'I think you selected number three. Am I correct?' And, believe it or not, most times you will be right. It does not work every time but most people will think of number three.

145. Psychological Number—2

Ask anyone to think of any number between one and ten.

Now tell them that they thought of seven and in most cases you will be correct.

146. Psychological Flower

Ask someone quickly to think of a flower.

Once again, it may not work every time, but you will find that most people will think of a rose.

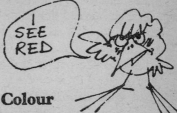

147. Psychological Colour

This time you ask someone to think, as quickly as they can, of a colour.

Nine times out of ten the selected colour will be red.

Like the other psychological tricks, this one does not work every time but when it does it appears to be genuine mindreading.

148. Coloured Thoughts

A packet of crayons

Someone selects one of the crayons and places it in your hands which are held behind your back. After a few seconds concentration you name the chosen colour.

As soon as the crayon is handed to you dig your right thumbnail into it. Now bring your right hand from behind your back (the crayon remains in the left hand) and place it to your forehead as if concentrating. All you have to do is to look at your thumbnail and you know what colour has been chosen.

149. Coincidence

Several coins, a hat or a box

Show some coins, all of which have different dates on them, and drop them into the box.

Now turn your back and ask someone to take out any one coin and remember its date. The coin is then to be handed around to several other people in the group so they, too, can look at the date. It is then dropped back into the box and the box is shaken up as you turn back around again.

You place your hand in the box and pick out a coin. It is the very same coin that was selected by the audience a few moments before!

How did you do it?

When you put your hand in the box you pick up several coins until you find one that is slightly warmer than the others. This is the selected coin because the number of people who handled it before it was replaced in the box have made it warmer. All the other coins will be cold.

Magic that Baffles

150. Funnel Fun

A funnel (or a cone of paper), a candle

Light the candle and hand the funnel to your victim. 'Blow the candle out by blowing through the funnel,' you order.

Most people will now put the narrow end of the funnel into their mouth and blow through it but that way the candle will never go out. When your friend has given up, take the funnel and blow through its widest end at the candle. The narrow end of the funnel directs all of your breath towards the candle and the flame will be extinguished.

151. Hole in the Hand

A sheet of paper

Roll the paper into a tube of about two centimetres diameter. Now look through the tube with your left eye and at your right hand, which is held palm uppermost by the side of the tube, with your right eye. It will appear that there is a gaping hole in the right hand through which you can see everything that is beyond it.

152. Coin and Bottle

A milk bottle, a coin

Place the coin on the table and then put the bottle on top of it. Now boast that you can pick up the coin without touching the bottle. Everyone will believe that it is impossible but all you have to do is to hit the side of the table with your hand. You may have to do this more than once but eventually the bottle will move off the coin sufficiently so that you can pick it up.

153. Cork Control

A cork, a glass or a cup, some water

Fill the glass until the water is about one centimetre from the brim. Give the cork to someone and ask him to place it in the water so that it floats exactly in the centre. He will find that it will not stay in the middle but will move to the side of the glass and stay there.

To make the cork move to the centre simply pour more water into the glass until it is absolutely full to the brim. As you do this the cork will move into the centre as if by magic.

154. Flexible Pencil

A pencil

Hold a pencil in a horizontal position between the thumb and forefinger of the right hand about two centimetres along from its blunt end. Holding the pencil fairly loosely, shake it up and down and, at the same time, move the hand up and down also. Look at the pencil now! It appears to be bending as if it is made of rubber.

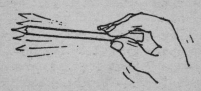

155. The Appearing Knot

A handkerchief

Before your performance secretly tie a knot in one end of the handkerchief.

When the time comes to demonstrate the trick, hold the hanky in your right hand by the knotted corner so that the knot is concealed in the hand. Point to the bottom corner and then lift it with the left hand and place it in the right hand. Shake the handkerchief and at the same time let go of the corner with the knot but keep hold of the other end.

All you have done is change ends but it appears that you have made a knot form in the handkerchief by magic.

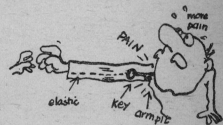

156. Key Vanish

A key, a safety pin, elastic

As you hand someone a key it vanishes!

The key is in fact tied to a piece of elastic that goes up your sleeve. The other end of the elastic is anchored with a safety pin.

Hold the key in your hand with your fingers covering the elastic. Ask someone to take it from you and as their hand comes towards you let go of the elastic and the key will fly up your sleeve. It appears to have vanished.

157 Brush Off

A coin, a soft hairbrush

Place the coin in the palm of your hand and give the hairbrush to a friend. Say: 'I bet that you can't brush this coin off my hand using only long and straight sweeps of the hairbrush.'

No matter how hard he tries the coin will remain on your hand.

158. Double Quantity

A glass of water, a lot of pins

Fill a glass to the brim with water (a wine glass is best). It is impossible to get anything else into the glass without spilling the water. Right?

Wrong!

If you carefully drop the pins into the glass one at a time you will find that you can get a great many of them into the glass before any water starts to spill.

It looks most uncanny.

159. Rainbow Production

Two sheets of glass, water

How can you make a rainbow? That's easy. All you have
to do is take two sheets of glass and stick them together
with water instead of glue. If you now hold the glass sheets
up to a candle flame or a light bulb you will be able to
see rainbow coloured fringes around the edges of the light
source.

160. Coin Count

Twelve coins

Hand a friend twelve coins with the challenge that he
cannot arrange them in rows on the table in such a way
that it is possible to count four coins in a straight line,
either horizontally or vertically, in any direction.

The secret is to place nine of the coins in three rows
of three to form a square and then to position the three
remaining coins as follows: The first goes on the first
coin of the first row, the second on the second coin of
the second row, and the third coin is placed upon the third
coin of the third row. There are now four coins in every
horizontal row and also four coins in every vertical row.

161. Pencil Power

A pencil

Would you like to make a pencil seem to stick to your hand? This is how you do it: Place the pencil on your right palm and grasp the right wrist with the left hand. Slowly turn the right hand over so that its back faces your audience and, at the same time, secretly raise your left forefinger behind the right hand to support the pencil. From the front it looks as if the pencil is stuck to your hand.

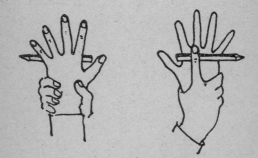

162. The Magnetised Pencil

A pencil, a pin

Before you show this trick to anyone you must first prepare the pencil by sticking the pin into it. If you now rest the pencil on your palm so that the pin goes in between your fingers you will find that by tightening your finger grip on the pin as you turn the hand over, the pencil will apparently adhere to your hand. You can show your hand on both sides but because the fingers conceal the pin no-one will be able to see how the trick is accomplished.

163. Curious Curves

Two pieces of curved card as shown in the illustration

Both pieces of curved card must be exactly the same size.
Colour the two pieces different colours.

If you place one curve above the other as shown in the
illustration it appears that the uppermost card is shorter
than the one below. Pretend to stretch the 'short' one and
then show them again but this time put the other card at
the top and that will now appear to be the shorter of the
two.

The whole trick is simply an optical illusion but it
looks like a piece of baffling magic.

164. Anti-gravity Balloon

A balloon

Inflate the balloon and rub
it on your jumper a few
times or, better still, rub
it vigorously with a nylon
duster. You will now find
that you can put the balloon
on a wall – and it will stay
there! Try it and see.

165. Stretching a handkerchief

A handkerchief

Show the handkerchief to your audience by holding it at the two top corners. Now take it by the diagonally opposite corners and twirl it between the hands into a sort of rope. At the same time bunch part of the handkerchief into each hand so that you are no longer holding it at the extreme corners but have several centimetres of material concealed in each fist.

Now twirl the handkerchief between the hands again and pretend to be stretching the material. Repeat this several times and the handkerchief will really appear to be getting longer. This action is quite effective just by itself but if you occasionally let out some of the material concealed in your hands it becomes even more convincing. Eventually you will finish up by holding the two ends (originally the two diagonally opposite corners) right at the fingertips and the spectators will be convinced that you have stretched the handkerchief to several times its original size.

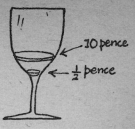

166. The Flying Coin

A half pence coin, a ten pence coin, a wineglass

Put the half pence coin in the bottom of the wine glass and then place the ten pence piece on top of it so that they are in the positions shown in the illustration. Can you now get the ½p out of the glass without touching either the glass or the coins?

Give up?

This is what you have to do. Just blow hard on one side of the 10p and it will swivel over as the ½p jumps out of the glass. It's easy when you know how, isn't it?

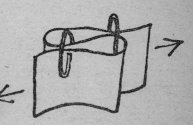

167. Clip Link

Paper, two paper clips

Fold a strip of paper into an S shape and put the paper clips on it in the positions shown in the illustration. Make sure that each clip goes over two thicknesses of paper only. Now pull the ends of the paper sharply apart and the clips will leap into the air. When they land you will find that they have linked themselves together.

168. Aristotle's Illusion

Two marbles

Show a friend two marbles and place them on the table in front of him. Tell him to close his eyes and cross the first and second fingers of one hand.

Now guide his hand so that the inner surfaces at the tips of the crossed fingers are touching one of the marbles. Quietly remove the other marble from the table.

Ask him how many marbles he can feel. Most people will say 'two'. Your friend will get quite a shock when he opens his eyes to find that there is only one marble beneath his fingers.

169. Amazing Arithmetic—1

It is worth remembering the calculations shown on this page. They will baffle your friends and amaze your teachers!

Here is the first one:

$$9 \times 9 + 7 = 88$$
$$98 \times 9 + 6 = 888$$
$$987 \times 9 + 5 = 8888$$
$$9876 \times 9 + 4 = 88888$$
$$98765 \times 9 + 3 = 888888$$
$$987654 \times 9 + 2 = 8888888$$
$$9876543 \times 9 + 1 = 88888888$$
$$98765432 \times 9 + 0 = 888888888$$

170. Amazing Arithmetic—2

$$1 \times 8 + 1 = 9$$
$$12 \times 8 + 2 = 98$$
$$123 \times 8 + 3 = 987$$
$$1234 \times 8 + 4 = 9876$$
$$12345 \times 8 + 5 = 98765$$
$$123456 \times 8 + 6 = 987654$$
$$1234567 \times 8 + 7 = 9876543$$
$$12345678 \times 8 + 8 = 98765432$$
$$123456789 \times 8 + 9 = 987654321$$

171. Amazing Arithmetic—3

$$1 \times 9 - 1 = 8$$
$$21 \times 9 - 1 = 188$$
$$321 \times 9 - 1 = 2888$$
$$4321 \times 9 - 1 = 38888$$
$$54321 \times 9 - 1 = 488888$$
$$654321 \times 9 - 1 = 5888888$$
$$7654321 \times 9 - 1 = 68888888$$
$$87654321 \times 9 - 1 = 788888888$$
$$987654321 \times 9 - 1 = 8888888888$$

172. Amazing Arithmetic—4

$$1 \times 9 + 2 = 11$$
$$12 \times 9 + 3 = 111$$
$$123 \times 9 + 4 = 1111$$
$$1234 \times 9 + 5 = 11111$$
$$12345 \times 9 + 6 = 111111$$
$$123456 \times 9 + 7 = 1111111$$
$$1234567 \times 9 + 8 = 11111111$$
$$12345678 \times 9 + 9 = 111111111$$

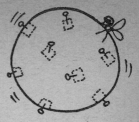

173. Invulnerable Balloon

A balloon, clear adhesive tape, pins

Stick pins into an unburstable balloon!

What you do not tell your friends is that you have secretly stuck some pieces of clear adhesive tape to the balloon.

Stick the pins into the balloon where the tape is. You will be able to see the tape but to your friends, who are further away, it's invisible.

174. Cunning Coin

A coin, a handkerchief, an accomplice

This is a really amazing trick if performed correctly and yet it is very easy to do.

You show a coin on your palm and cover it with a handkerchief. Several members of the audience are allowed to feel beneath the handkerchief to reassure themselves that it is still there. In spite of the precautions, when the hanky is lifted the coin has vanished.

You now replace the hanky over your hand and allow people to feel beneath the hanky to make sure that the hand remains empty. Yet when you lift the handkerchief again the coin has mysteriously returned.

The secret is very simple. The last person to feel beneath the handkerchief each time is your friend. On the first occasion, instead of just feeling the coin, he takes it out of your hand and the next time around he puts it back. It is as simple as that and yet it can be very baffling to people who do not know how it is done.

175. Pin Puzzler

A pin, a glass tumbler, some water, a strong magnet

Fill the tumbler with water and drop the pin into it. Now challenge someone to get the pin out of the glass without getting his fingers wet and without pouring the water away or drinking it.

When he gives up you place the tumbler behind your back (so that no-one can see what you do), remove the magnet from your back pocket where you secreted it earlier, and slide the magnet up the side of the glass. The pin will be attracted to the magnet and will slide up and out of the water. Remove the pin from the magnet, drop the magnet back in your pocket, and then show that you have accomplished yet another miracle for the pin is out of the water, your hands are dry, and the water is still in the tumbler.

176. All Tied Up

Two handkerchiefs, a small elastic band

Place the elastic band over the tips of the thumb and first finger of the right hand. The audience must not know about the elastic band so it must be positioned on the fingertips secretly before you show the trick.

Pick up one of the handkerchiefs and place it in your right hand, really putting the end of it into the elastic band. Do the same with the second hanky. Throw the handkerchiefs into the air, allowing the band to slip off the fingers at the same time. As the hankies flutter to the ground catch one of them, and the elastic band holding them together makes it look as if they have tied themselves together in mid-air.

177. Ring on String

A length of string, a ring or bangle

First of all, the ends of the string should be tied together to form a loop. Have a friend extend his hands and place the string over his forefingers as shown in the illustration.

The trick is to get the ring on the string without removing the loop from your friend's fingers, It sounds impossible but it can be done.

First pull a loop of the string towards you and thread the ring on to it as shown in the drawing. Now place loop A over your friend's second finger, remove loop B from his first finger and the trick is done.

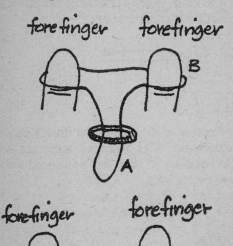

178. Give it a Scratch

Two large coins, one small coin, a tumbler

The table on which you perform this trick must have a cloth on it.

Place the three coins in a row on the table with the smallest coin in the centre. Put the tumbler upside down so that its edge rests upon the two large coins as shown in the drawing.

Now challenge someone to remove the small coin from beneath the tumbler without touching any of the coins or the glass.

When he gives up all you have to do is to scratch the cloth in front of the glass. Keep scratching and the small coin will slowly walk out all by itself!

179. The Walking Hairpin

A hairpin, a ruler

Ask your mother for the loan of a hairpin and then show her this little trick.

Place the hairpin over the ruler and then, holding the end of the ruler in one hand, lower the pin until its 'feet' touch the tabletop.

If the top of the hairpin is leaning toward you it will now walk, as if by magic, towards you. If it is leaning the other way it will walk away from you of its own accord.

To make the hairpin walk even faster just tilt the ruler slightly – down if you want it to come to you and up if you want it to go away.

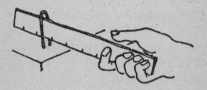

180. The Watertight Sieve

A bottle of water, a sieve

A sieve that will not let water pass through it? That's impossible!

Not if you do it this way.

Fill a milk bottle with water. Put the sieve over the mouth of the bottle and then turn the whole lot upside down keeping the sieve and the bottle in contact all the time. It must be magic for the water does not run out.

NOTE. DO THIS TRICK OVER THE SINK

GIRLS WHO DO
THIS TRICK
SHOULD MAKE SURE
THAT THEY WEAR
SOMETHING BELTED
AT THE WAIST.

181. Coin Vanish

A coin

This is really only suitable for showing to one person at a time.

Have him stand facing you and ask him to hold out one hand. Remove the coin from your pocket and say that, on the count of three, you are going to place the coin in his hand and he is to close his hand as quickly as he can.

Hold your hand, with the coin, out in front of you and then bring the coin down to touch his palm. Count 'One'. Lift the hand a little higher than before and bring it down again to his palm. Count 'Two'. Again lift your hand but this time you lift it so high that your hand comes up to your shoulder. At this precise moment you drop the coin into your collar but without stopping bring the hand down to the spectator's palm. In accordance with your instructions, he closes his hand.

Your hand is empty – but so is his. The coin has vanished.

When doing this trick keep your eyes on the spectator's hand and he will be looking down as well.

Make sure you wear something belted at the waist otherwise the coin may fall through your clothing and on to the floor.

182. Topsy-Turvy Pound

A pound note, or a piece of paper with writing on it

Take the note and fold it in half lengthways.

Now fold it in half the other way but fold the right half backwards as shown in the illustration.

Fold it in half again but this time fold the right half towards you.

Open out all the folds from the front and the note has turned upside down.

Once you get the hang of it this trick is really quite simple – but it looks amazing.

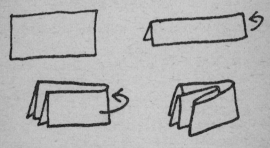

183. Stringed Ring

A piece of string, a large ring

Tie the ends of the string together so that it forms a loop. Get someone to hold up their thumbs and loop the string on to them. Lift off one end of the loop, thread the ring on the string, and then replace it over the person's thumb.

Now challenge the person to get the ring off the string without removing the string from her thumbs.

Some people will actually manage to do this – by accident, but most will not have a clue. In fact all you have to do is lower one hand so that the ring slides down the string and on to the thumb. It's as simple as that.

184. Hovercard

A cotton reel, two pieces of card, a pin, glue

Glue a small square of card to the end of the cotton reel. With a pencil make a hole in this card to coincide with the hole in the centre of the reel.

Push the pin through the centre of the second square of card, which is bigger than the first piece.

Now place the cotton reel on top of the large card so that the pin sticks up into the hole as shown in the drawing.

Show this to your friends and challenge them to pick up the large card without touching it and without sucking through the cotton reel.

The answer to this little problem is to *blow* through the hole in the centre of the reel.

Try it and see.

185. It's a Hold Up

A brick wall, someone who is easily fooled

You need a really gullible friend for this trick. As he or she approaches you in the street put both your hands against a brick wall and push hard as if you are trying to stop it falling over. When your friend reaches you say: 'Can you just hold this for me for a minute,' and get him to push against the wall also.

As soon as your friend is holding up the wall you carefully remove your hands so that he is now apparently holding the wall up all by himself.

And then you walk away and leave him to it!

186. A Weighty Problem

Pencil, paper

Get two pieces of paper, both the same shape and size. On one of them write the word LIGHT and on the other write HEAVY.

Now say to your friends: 'If I drop both these papers at exactly the same time I bet that the paper with "heavy" on it will reach the ground first.' Your mates will reason that, as both papers are the same size and weight, they will reach the ground at more or less the same time.

But they will be wrong.

You drop both papers and the 'heavy' paper falls straight to the ground whereas the 'light' paper floats gently down.

How?

You cheat – that's how!

Just before you drop the papers screw the 'heavy' one into a ball and it will fall quicker than the other one.

187. Sleight of Hand

Two small coins

Place one coin on the palm of the left hand and the other coin on the first and second fingers of the right hand as shown in the illustration. The hands are rested on a table, palms uppermost, about eighteen centimetres apart.

Quickly turn the hands over towards each other but without lifting them from the table. The audience will think that there is one coin beneath each hand but when you lift the right hand there is nothing there. Both coins are found under the left hand.

People will think that you are an expert at sleight of hand but in fact, if you position the coins correctly, the trick works by itself. As you turn the hands over the left coin stays beneath the left hand but the right coin is automatically thrown across to join the one in the left hand.

Although this trick works by itself it is a good idea to practise it in private first before you show it to anyone.

188. One Hundred Wins

Pencil, paper

Challenge someone to a simple game. All he has to do is to write down any number from one to ten, then you do the same and add the two numbers together. You continue with each of you adding a number to the total alternately. The object of the game is to reach one hundred and the person who calls out the final number to make the sum come to one hundred is the winner. This can be you every time for you know a little secret that the other person does not.

All you have to do is make sure that the total hits one of the following numbers: 12, 23, 34, 45, 56, 67, 78, 89. These are easier to remember if you think of them as one two, two three, three four, four five, and so on. Once you have managed to hit one of these numbers all you have to do is call numbers that added to the spectator's previous number will make eleven. Once you reach 89 it does not matter what number he calls for you can easily make the total reach one hundred – and you are the winner.

189. Handkerchief Vanisher

A handkerchief, a coin, a small elastic band

Secretly place the elastic band around the thumb and fingers of your left hand. The audience must not be aware of this secret preparation.

Show the handkerchief and place it over the left hand and, of course, over the elastic band. As you take a coin from your pocket with your right hand, open the fingers of the left hand beneath the hanky, stretching the elastic.

Place the coin on the centre of the hanky and then allow the elastic band to slip off the fingers so that it forms a little bag in the handkerchief enclosing the coin. You will now find that you can shake the hanky quite vigorously and the coin, which is hidden in the secret pocket at the back, has apparently disappeared.

Casually replace the hanky in your pocket and the trick is complete.

190. Pinpointed

Two safety pins

Link two safety pins together and hold them as shown in the illustration. If you now part your hands you will find that the pin held in the right hand will cause the left hand pin to open and then close again and that the two pins are now apart. It may take a bit of practice to get the exact movement to cause this to happen but once you have you will find that it appears to the spectators that one pin has penetrated the other.

191. Colour-Changing Balloon

Two balloons of different colours, a pin

The magician (that's you!) comes on to the stage holding an inflated blue balloon. Suddenly there is a bang and the balloon has changed to red!

Two balloons are used, the red one being inside the blue one. Blow up the inner balloon and tie the neck. Before tying the neck of the outer balloon put a bit more air into it so that there will be a small gap between the two balloons.

You show the blue balloon and then secretly burst it with the pin concealed in your hand. The outer balloon disintegrates to reveal the inner balloon. To the audience it appears that the balloon has changed colour.

When bursting the outer balloon be careful that the pin does not go through both balloons!

192. Magic Ring

Two large identical rings or bangles, a piece of string

Before performing this trick place one of the bangles on your arm and then push it up your sleeve so that it is out of sight.

Show your audience the second ring and the length of string and ask someone to tie the string to each of your wrists. You now take the ring, turn your back for a moment, and when you turn back to face the spectators they will be amazed to see that the ring is now hanging on the string.

What actually happens when you turn your back is that you place the second ring in your pocket and pull down the concealed ring over your hand and on to the string. As the audience is aware of only one ring being used for the trick they think that you somehow caused it to penetrate the string.

193. Vanishing Water

A glass of water, a friend with a drinking straw

This trick is best performed in a room containing several people. Choose one of them and offer to show a baffling magic trick. Have him sit on a chair in the centre of the room. Give him the glass of water and tell him to hold it on top of his head. He is to use both hands for this.

Now, keep talking.

While you are talking your friend creeps up behind the seated person, puts the straw into the glass, and drinks the water through the straw. He then creeps away again, taking the straw with him.

Now ask the seated person to remove the glass of water from his head. He will have quite a surprise when he finds that the water has vanished.

194. Quick Knot

A piece of string

Hold a piece of string exactly as shown in the first illustration. Bring your hands together and take the two opposite ends of the string in the fingers as shown in the second picture. Pull the hands apart and a knot appears in the centre of the string.

Practise this until you can do it easily and quickly so that the knot seems to appear by magic and you will have a trick that will really baffle people.

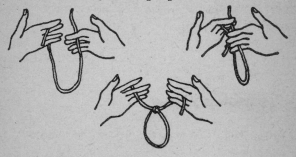

195. Portrait Painter

Pencil, paper, someone to draw

Hold up the pencil and the paper and say to a friend. 'I am a great artist and I am going to draw a portrait of you.'

When the drawing is finished you show it to your subject. He or she may not be very impressed because all you have drawn is a large letter U.

196. Card Spring

A glass tumbler, a playing card, soap

You remove a playing card from the pack and place it into a glass tumbler. As soon as you release your hold on the card it jumps upward as if by magic.

Soap, not magic, does the trick for you. Before your performance draw two lines with the soap on the inner walls of the tumbler directly opposite one another. When you place the card into the glass make sure that its edges are right on top of the soaped lines. Push the card down with your fingers and as soon as you leave go the card will spring up the slippery sides of the glass.

If someone else wants to have a go make sure that the card is placed in the glass so that its edges are not touching the soaped lines.

197. Mad Maths

Paper, pencil

'One hundred plus eleven makes 199.'

When you say this to your friends they will say, 'You can't add up. One hundred plus eleven equals 111.'

But you can prove that your statement was correct.

Write down the number like this:

100

Make the noughts small as above. Now add the eleven like this:

199

And you have proved that one hundred plus eleven equals 199.

198. In the Post

A pillar box, the ability to act

'Are you all right? Well, just a minute and I will find someone to let you out.' People will begin to stop and stare when they hear you saying that to a pillar box – yes, a pillar box!

As the crowd gathers you continue your conversation with the imaginary person inside the letter box: 'How did you get in there in the first place?' Pretend to hear a reply, then say, 'Well that was a silly thing to do. I will go and telephone the Post Office. Whatever you do, keep your mouth closed when someone posts a letter or you might swallow it.'

Now walk away as if going to the telephone. By this time the crowd will be so curious that someone is bound to look into the pillar box to see if there really is someone in there!

199. Point the other way

A postcard, pencil, glass tumbler, some water

Fold the postcard in half and draw an arrow on the top half. Stand the card on a table so that the arrow is visible. Place the glass tumbler about five centimetres in front of the card. Look through the glass at the arrow and it will obviously be pointing in the direction you drew. Now pour some water in the glass and look again. The arrow appears to be pointing in the opposite direction.

200. Multiplying Money

Ten coins, a magazine

Secretly hide three coins inside the cover of the magazine, place the magazine on the table, and you are ready to perform this amazing trick.

Show your audience seven coins. Casually pick up the magazine and count the coins on to it, one by one. Now bend the magazine up into a U-shape so that you can easily tip the coins into someone's hand. At the same time, of course, the three hidden coins will slip out from beneath the cover into the spectator's hand although he is not aware of this.

Ask him to close his hand over the coins and you will show him how to make money increase in quantity. Ask him to concentrate for a second or two and then to open his hand. Much to his amazement he will now find that the seven coins are now ten!

Answers

16. The paragraph does not include the letter 'e', which is the most common letter in the English language.

32. Instead of pulling the cork out of the bottle, push it in to get the coin out. Sneaky, eh?

has a whole shipload of exciting books for you

Here are just some of the best-selling titles that Armada has to offer: